A History of Fashion and Costume

The Medieval World

Philip Steele

☑® Facts On File, Inc.

The Medieval World

Copyright © 2005 Bailey Publishing Associates Ltd

Produced for Facts On File by
Bailey Publishing Associates Ltd
11a Woodlands
Hove BN3 6TJ

Project Manager: Roberta Bailey
Editor: Alex Woolf
Text Designer: Simon Borrough
Artwork: Dave Burroughs, Peter Dennis,
Tony Morris
Picture Research: Glass Onion Pictures

Printed and bound in China

Facts On File, Inc.
132 West 31st Street
New York NY 10001

Facts On File books are available at special
discounts when purchased in bulk quantities for
businesses, associations, institutions, or sales
promotions. Please call our Special Sales
Department in New York at 212/967-8800 or
800/322-8755.

You can find Facts On File on the World Wide
Web at: http://www.factsonfile.com

Library of Congress Cataloging-in-Publication Data

Steele, Philip, 1948–
A history of fashion and costume.
   The medieval world/Philip Steele.
   p. cm.
Includes bibliographical references and
index.

ISBN 0-8160-5945-4
   1. Clothing and dress—History—
Medieval, 500–1500
   GT575.S84 2005
   391/.009/02—dc 22   2004060891

The publishers would like to thank the
following for permission to use their
pictures:

Art Archive: 7, 8, 9, 10, 11, 14. 15
(both), 16, 19, 21, 22, 25 (bottom), 26,
27, 28, 30, 32, 33, 34, 35, 36, 37, 39, 40,
41, 43, 45, 47, 48 (top), 49, 51, 53 (top),
54 (both), 55, 56, 57, 58, 59
Werner Forman Archive: 12, 13, 25
(top), 38, 48 (bottom), 53 (bottom)

Contents

Introduction

The costumes of the Middle Ages still fascinate us. Children's fairytale books are filled with fanciful pictures of European princesses in tall "steeple" hats, of honest woodcutters in homespun cloth, of knights in shining armor, and colorful court jesters. Medieval costume inspired romantic poets and artists of the nineteenth century, as well as the makers of fantasy films in the twenty-first. The reality of medieval costume is every bit as interesting as the fantasy.

Finding Out

How do we discover the truth about the way people dressed in the medieval period? Firstly, actual items of jewelry, crowns, shoes, suits of armor, and the remains of textiles have survived. The latter may be fragments of cloth uncovered by archaeologists, or they may be whole garments now preserved in a palace or museum. Secondly, there are visual references supplied by statues, memorial brasses in churches, paintings, or illustrated manuscripts. Thirdly, we have descriptions of clothing in medieval literature, or references to it in other written records such as laws, tax receipts, or trading accounts.

When and Where?

The term "Middle Ages" strictly refers to the period of European history between the classical and the modern age. It begins with the fall of the Roman Empire in the west, in 476 CE, and may be said to end with the fall of the eastern Roman, or Byzantine, Empire in 1453. It is sometimes extended to include the Renaissance, the cultural reawakening which began in southern Europe and continued into the mid-sixteenth century.

This book deals broadly with the period 500 to 1550 CE and looks beyond the frontiers of Europe to the Silk Road, the ancient trading route between China and the West. It visits the dye pits of Kano in West Africa and crosses the Indian and Pacific Oceans. It describes the dress of the Incas in Peru and the feather craftworkers of Aztec Mexico.

Costume does not just reveal ideas about beauty or fashion. It tells us about craft, technology, politics and power, social classes, religion, customs, childhood, and the world of work. It is the key to a bygone age.

Chapter 1: Europe 500–1000

Raiders and Riders

When the Roman Empire finally collapsed in 476 CE, Germanic tribes such as the Angles, Saxons, and Franks were already invading much of western Europe. The incomers were warriors and their dress was practical, designed for riding and battle, for farming, or for building new settlements, rather than for affairs of state, business, or leisure.

This Anglo-Saxon ceremonial helmet, from Sutton Hoo in England, dates from about 625. It shows Roman influence in its design.

Troubled Times

The early Middle Ages in Europe have sometimes been called the Dark Ages. There was almost constant warfare, lawlessness, and a lack of stable government. This led to the disruption of education, and only limited historical records have survived. However, the artistic inspiration and high craft standards of peoples such as the Angles, Saxons, Irish, or Vikings, seen for example in their surviving jewelry, suggest that this age was far from barbaric.

Kingdoms and Empires

In eastern and central Europe, there were invasions by Slavs from southern Russia, and Magyars (Hungarians) from Asia. However, the city of Constantinople or Byzantium (modern Istanbul), capital of the Byzantine Empire, did not fall to invaders. The empire offered all the pomp and glitter of an imperial court and provided a living for all sorts of people, including officials, lawyers, teachers, merchants, priests, laborers, and organizers of horse races.

By the seventh and eighth centuries, new, small kingdoms were being founded across western Europe, and in 800 the Frankish ruler Charlemagne was crowned ruler of an empire which stretched from the Pyrenean Mountains, on the borders of Spain, to central Europe. Western Europe, now mostly Christian, was becoming a more settled society.

The Social Background

To understand how people dressed in the Middle Ages, we need to know how society was organized. The feudal system was developing at this time—a social order based on oaths of service. Kings granted large areas of land to their nobles in return for their loyalty and military support. Workers promised to supply labor, military service, and produce to the nobles in return for military protection or a roof over their heads. Increasingly, the superior status of the nobles was emphasized by their dress, quality of cloth, and styles of fashion.

Early Medieval Textiles

Woolen cloth was processed by hand. Raw wool was carded (combed out) and then wound onto a handheld cleft stick, called a distaff. From here it was drawn out with the fingers onto a drop spindle, a suspended rod about eight inches (20 cm) long, fitted with a disk called a whorl. The whorl kept the spindle revolving evenly. The pull of gravity drew the thread downward as it was twisted by the spindle. Thread could then be wound into a skein, for coloring with natural dyes.

The woody stems of the flax plant were stripped, dried, and then soaked in water to extract the fiber inside. This could be spun and woven to make linen, which was cooler and smoother than wool. Another plant, hemp, could be processed to make a cheaper, scratchier cloth, sometimes used by poor people. Cotton was still a rare import for most of Europe.

A reconstruction at Jorvik, the Viking settlement of York, in England, shows the vertical warp-weighted loom in use at the time.

A Viking Loom

The Vikings were Scandinavian sea raiders, who attacked and settled the coasts of western Europe in the ninth century. Their looms, or weaving frames, leaned upright against the walls of their houses. The upright, or warp, threads were kept taut at the base by stone or clay weights and were separated by a horizontal bar called a heddle. The horizontal, or weft, threads were passed through the gap in the warp and then beaten upwards with a long batten made of wood, iron, or whalebone. Weaving was done in the home.

State and Church

The Frankish emperor Charlemagne, who lived from 747 to 814, is shown here both as crowned head of state and as a man of action.

The Byzantine emperor Justinian I, who died in 565, wears a crown with pendants and a purple robe.

The warrior bands of the early Middle Ages would be led by a chieftain or warlord, who might own better weapons or armor than his followers, but who wore no special clothes to indicate his rank. However, when kingdoms and empires were founded, the descendants of those chieftains had much grander ideas of their own importance. The tombstone of Cadfan, seventh-century ruler of Gwynedd, a small kingdom in North Wales, describes him as "the wisest and most renowned of all kings." The high status now enjoyed by even minor royalty was reinforced by their costume.

Crowned Heads

The royal crowns of the early Middle Ages derived from royal circlets or diadems worn in Persia, which were adopted by the Byzantine emperors and empresses. These crowns included pendants, jeweled pieces hanging down on each side of the face. Kings of the Visigoths, a Germanic people who ruled Spain in the 600s, wore circlets of thick gold set with pearls and precious stones. Two centuries later, Charlemagne's crown was made up of gold plaques set with sapphires and emeralds and decorated with enameled figures from the Bible. Many crowns were topped with crosses, emphasizing that the king ruled by the will of God.

Robes and Jewels

Western European kings looked eastward to the splendor of the Byzantine Empire. Its powerful emperor wore a long under-tunic with a looser, shorter outer tunic. The cloth was of silk, embroidered with gold thread. The Byzantine empress wore a long tunic with a richly embroidered collar and stole, studded with gems. As in ancient Rome, purple was the color reserved for the imperial family. Other European rulers also began to wear long robes for state occasions, and decorated their clothes with jewels.

Regalia

Medieval rulers wore or carried all sorts of emblems, called regalia (royal things), to emphasize their status as representatives of the state. These included cloaks, rings, scepters, orbs, swords, bracelets, gloves and, most importantly, crowns. The full royal costume would be worn at coronations and important state occasions. Medieval kings were frequently in the saddle, hunting or fighting battles, and at such times their long robes would be replaced by more practical tunics, cloaks, or shirts of mail.

Religious Dress

Early Christian monks and priests wore similar tunics and cloaks to everyone else. However, religious costume, like royal dress, soon developed symbolic meanings. In Rome and Constantinople, bishops and popes dressed to show that their authority came from God. Their dress

became very grand. Wide, T-shaped tunics called dalmatics were of the same design as those worn by kings for their coronations. Bishops in the Celtic Church wore crowns. Clergy wore long, white tunics called albs beneath sleeveless mantles called chasubles. Long stoles or scarves would be embroidered with the sign of the cross.

The appearance of the clergy led to many heated debates in the early Middle Ages. Monks in the Catholic Church of Rome shaved a circular patch from their hair as a symbol of the crown of thorns worn by Jesus. However, monks in the Celtic Church shaved a band across their hair from ear to ear, a custom which probably dated back to the druids, the Celtic priests of the pre-Christian age. The Catholic Church ruled that this tonsure (method of shaving) was unholy. Between the seventh and twelfth centuries the Celtic Church was absorbed into the Roman tradition.

Deacons of the Church lead the Byzantine empress Theodora (500–548) to worship. She wears a crown and imperial robes under a gem-studded collar.

Chieftains, Lords, and Ladies

In the early Middle Ages the upper classes were chiefly distinguished by the quality of the cloth they wore, by embroidered hems and cuffs, and by fine dyes. Broad bands of color were popular among nobles of northern Europe.

Tunics and Trousers

The linen or woolen tunic was the basis of dress across most of Europe for all social classes and both sexes. The long tunics and robes of the Roman Empire were still seen at the royal court or in church, but shorter, knee-length tunics were now worn by noblemen, often with breeches. These might be bound around the calves with crisscrossed thongs or worn with knee-length laced boots or shoes of soft leather.

Most noblewomen also wore tunics, with designs that varied with time and place. In seventh-century Spain

Byzantine noble, 600

the tunic might be more like a dress, shaped and close-fitting with long sleeves. In eighth-century France a looser, calf-length tunic, with three-quarter-length sleeves, might be worn over a long shift. Long stoles or scarves could be draped gracefully over the shoulders or head. Noblewomen wore delicate shoes of soft leather or embroidered linen.

Girdles and Cloaks

Tunics for both sexes were generally gathered with a girdle or belt, which might be a strip of fancy leather or embroidered cloth. Men might wear an ornate buckle or a sheath for a knife on their belt, while a woman's girdle often supported a satchel, as there were no pockets in their garments. Sometimes women wore a broad sash around the hips, knotted and hanging down at the front.

Byzantine Silks

Silk was the most luxurious cloth of all. The breeding of silkworms and the spinning and weaving of this shimmering textile had originally been a secret of the Chinese, but had gradually spread southward and westward across Asia. The Greeks and Romans knew about silk, but the first serious attempt at creating a European silk industry began at Constantinople in the reign of Justinian I (c. 482–565 CE). Manufacture took place under high security, within the palace walls, and was of a very high standard. The best quality cloth was reserved for the emperor, but the courtiers also wore fine silk. Manufacture and trade were strictly controlled by the imperial court.

French
lady, 850

Anglo-Saxon
noble, 950

Even the finest palaces of the early Middle Ages were drafty places, and the wooden halls of a prince or chieftain in northern Europe must have been bitterly cold in winter. Warm cloaks of wool, fur, or hide were a necessity.

Jewelry

Cloaks for men and women were generally fastened at the shoulder or the chest by a round brooch secured with a long pin. The brooch was often the most elaborate and beautiful item worn. One of the most splendid examples is the "Tara" brooch, made in Ireland in the early eighth century. It is crafted from silver, bronze, glass, and amber, and even the back of the brooch—which would not have been seen when worn—is as lavishly decorated as the front.

Brooches, buckles, pins, necklaces, and earrings of this period show a high degree of craftsmanship. The Viking chieftains of the ninth century had some very fine examples made for themselves, and they also traded or plundered jewelry on their sea voyages. Hoards of Viking treasure, buried for safekeeping, reveal high-quality gold jewelry from all over Europe and the Middle East.

Enamelled brooch used to fasten cloaks. It was found in the bed of the River Shannon, in Ireland.

Working Clothes

In the Roman Empire, most laborers and slaves wore knee-length tunics, the most practical dress for plowing, fishing, or building a house. For greater mobility, the hem of the tunic could be drawn through the legs and tucked up into the belt, similar to a baby's diaper. This continued to be normal working dress during the early medieval period in southern Europe.

Cloths and Dyes

Tunics for slaves, or the poorest in society, were made of the coarsest woolen, linen, or hemp cloth. These were undyed. However, middle-class people, such as merchants, wore homespun cloth of a better quality. This might be dyed with the extracts of flowers, leaves, roots, or bark. Natural dyes included a plant called woad, which gave a blue color; a wildflower called weld, or dyer's rocket, which produced yellow; and madder, an evergreen shrub of the Mediterranean region, whose root produced a crimson dye.

Heavy-duty Clothing

The waterlogged clay of northern Europe required heavier plows than the lighter soils of the south. Northern farming was generally muddier, wetter, and colder, so people dressed accordingly. As well as the tunic, short breeches or longer trousers were generally worn, the latter often tied with thongs. Shoes of calfskin or goatskin were tightened with leather laces. Soles would be replaced when worn out, and sometimes shoes were fitted with wooden soles, like clogs. Knee-length boots and gaiters tied to linen trousers were also worn, although bare legs and feet were common among the poorest citizens.

Women at Work

A woman's work in a ninth-century Viking settlement was fairly typical of this age. It might include cooking, fetching water, and looking after livestock. When summer came and the men sailed off to raid foreign shores, the women stayed behind to run the household and often the farm as well. A lot of time was spent spinning, weaving, and making clothes for the family. A Viking woman would wear a long shift of wool or linen, with a sleeveless woolen tunic over the top. This was secured with shoulder straps fastened by brooches. Keys, pins, or other useful items were often kept on

A simple tunic remained the working dress of the plowman during most of the Middle Ages.

chains which hung from these brooches.

Everyday Accessories

Clothes were not made with pockets. Instead, pouches or purses of cloth or leather were attached to belts in order to hold money, hair combs, or other small or precious items. Not all jewelry was made of costly silver or gold. In northern Europe, antler horn, walrus tusk, bone, wood, glass beads, and stones such as jet, readily found on some beaches, were made into very beautiful ornaments.

Hats were a rare sight in the early Middle Ages. Simple cloth caps in the "Phrygian" style of the ancient Greeks were sometimes worn. These

were conical, with the peak flopping forward in the front. There were also broad-brimmed straw sunhats.

Viking women's dress was home-made, simple, practical and often colorful. Hair was worn long or tied back. Married women wore headscarves.

All Wrapped Up

Most people who wished to protect themselves from rain or snow would simply raise their cloaks to cover their heads. The cloak could also be wrapped around the body to serve as bedding for a weary traveler or a Viking seafarer. Woolen cloaks soon became soaked through with rain or spray, but cloaks of hide could offer some waterproofing. Iceland, colonized by Vikings in 874, became famous for exporting shaggy woolen cloaks. In eastern Europe, Bulgarian sheepskin coats became popular, worn with the fleecy side against the body.

Viking shoes were generally made of goat- or calf-skin and were either slippers or laced around the ankle.

Dressing for War

This decorative helmet, with an iron cap, would have been a highly prized possession. It was found in a burial at Vendel in Sweden, and probably dates from the second half of the seventh century.

After the collapse of the Roman Empire in the west, large standing armies rarely took to the battlefield. Much of the military action was now carried out by small, mobile bands of mounted warriors. Most were ordinary working people who owed allegiance to a local chieftain or lord.

They wore simple jerkins or tunics with breeches. A leather belt carried a scabbard for the sword. Little armor was worn. Some stitched metal plates onto their clothes for protection, but only the leaders owned helmets or mail shirts. The early Franks piled up their hair in braids to provide padded protection for their heads.

It was much the same with the Viking raiders of the ninth century. Their simple, conical helmets were made of iron or hardened leather. Some had nasals (bars to protect the nose). A few leading warriors had helmets with cheek guards or ornate protection for the face. The elite Viking shock troops were known as berserkers, or "wearers of bearskin shirts." They would work themselves up into a blood-crazed frenzy before battle. We still talk of people in a rage "going berserk."

Armies of Empire

The more orderly, large-scale military activities familiar to the ancient Romans lived on in the Byzantine Empire, which succeeded in recapturing former Roman territory in Italy and North Africa. However, the old Roman-style legions—large units of well-trained professional soldiers—had been disbanded. The Byzantine Empire was really a land of merchants, and its rulers

Shirts of Mail

Mail was a form of armor invented by the Celts sometime before the fifth century BCE. The Roman legions, who adopted the use of mail, called it *macula* (mesh), and this became the French word *maille*. Mail was made up of small, interlinking iron rings, riveted or pressed together and shaped into shirts, and later other forms of garment. In the early Middle Ages only a few warriors could afford shirts of mail, but from the ninth century onward it became increasingly common.

preferred to hire mercenaries to fight for them rather than raise their own armies. The Byzantine foot soldiers wore scale armor—tunics of sewn metal plates—over breeches. By the reign of Basil II (976–1025), the emperor was protected by an elite bodyguard of Rus (Swedish Vikings who had settled in Russia). They were known as the Varangian Guard and wore elaborate armor.

In the early ninth century, the armies of the Frankish emperor Charlemagne marched into battle wearing tunics with cloaks or kilts, similar to the style of the old Roman legions. Their helmets were either rounded or conical with a ridge along the crest.

Rise of the Knight

In the eighth century, a new invention called the stirrup reached Europe, which had originated three centuries earlier in China. By securing a horse rider's foot, the stirrup allowed him to stay in the saddle during the shattering impact of a cavalry charge. By the tenth century, heavy cavalry was

becoming increasingly important in warfare. The age of the knight was about to begin, and with it would come many social changes. These altered the way people dressed, and not just on the battlefield.

Carolingian soldier, c.800

Angevin knight, c.1125

Chapter 2: Europe 1000–1400

The feudal system in Europe reached its high point from the eleventh to the thirteenth centuries. Increasingly, the manners, costumes, and even language of the nobility differed from those of the common people who served, labored, and fought for them. By the 1300s, feudalism had begun to decline. Bankers and merchants—especially those engaged in the cloth trade—often became wealthier and sometimes more powerful than their feudal lords.

A German manuscript of 1305–40 shows a grand tournament. Even the fashions of the noble women spectators are outshone by the gaudy coats-of-arms and crests displayed by the knights.

The Age of Knights

Land and Power

In the eleventh century, as the power of the Byzantine Empire began to wane, the Holy Roman Empire—a loose federation of Germanic states which had replaced the eastern part of Charlemagne's old empire—prevailed in Europe. The Holy Roman Empire extended from Bohemia and Austria to the Netherlands.

Warfare still dominated all aspects of life. The mounted warriors, the knights, formed a new social elite. Tournaments, which were mock battles between knights, became a colorful showcase for the latest fashions. Long wars were fought to enlarge existing kingdoms or to conquer neighboring states. Other wars were fought between kings and rebel barons, who wanted regional power.

Textiles and Technology

At the height of the Middle Ages, textiles became a mainstay of the European economy. In England, more and more land was given over to sheep pasture for wool production. Flanders (modern Belgium) saw rapid growth in the woolen and linen trade, bringing huge wealth to its merchants. High-quality linen was also produced in France, and silk in Italy. Cotton appeared in Moorish Spain, and by the fourteenth century it was also being woven in northern Europe.

All commercial aspects of the textile industry were managed by trading organizations called guilds. These representatives of the craftspeople and merchants controlled prices, marketing, and the training of apprentices. The Guild of Weavers in London was founded in the early 1100s. At this time, spinning was considered to be woman's work and weaving was left to the men.

By the eleventh century, looms were mostly horizontal frames rather than upright posts. In the 1100s, treadles were added. These were foot-operated levers, a Chinese invention which moved the heddle mechanically and raised alternate warp threads in sequence. The yarn was passed through the gap, or shed, by a hand-operated shuttle, which contained a bobbin or reel of thread. Spinning wheels, originally an Indian or Chinese invention, first appeared in Europe in about 1200 and were in common use from the 1300s. They had a fixed distaff and wheel-driven spindle.

Eastern Luxury

The high Middle Ages were marked by conflict between Christianity and Islam. Beginning in 1095, religious orders of knights were formed to fight against Muslims in a long and brutal series of wars called the Crusades. These clashes did have some unexpected outcomes, with Muslim and Christian cultures frequently influencing each other. This happened in the Middle East, where Christian knights founded the Crusader states of Outremer in the eleventh century. In the Kingdom of Jerusalem, young knights from northern Europe first came across the luxuries of Asia. Many of them

adopted Asian dress, wearing long tunics and robes, pointed slippers, cloth-of-gold and silk, and turbans on their heads. This exotic dress influenced tastes back home in Europe, as did imports from Moorish kingdoms in Spain and North Africa, and from the Byzantine Empire.

A French illustration of the high Middle Ages shows women carding wool, spinning and weaving.

By 1400 the knight's mail was covered in sections of plate armor. Here it is being adjusted by the knight's squire, who is training to be a knight himself.

Ermine and Miters

During the Middle Ages, religious dress for men and women became a series of uniforms, which were rich in symbolic meaning.

The kings of the high Middle Ages continued to wear long tunics and robes in the Byzantine tradition. The style of royal dress varied within this period. For example, royal robes became extremely long in the early 1100s, and had to be gathered up at the waist. Long cuffs covered the hands. Queens wore state robes of the richest cloths and finest furs. The fashionable headdresses of the day were combined with circlets or full crowns.

The Royal Mantle

A large cloak or mantle, trimmed with fur, was an emblem of royalty and noble status. One of the most highly rated furs was ermine, made from the fur of the stoat. The coat of this little animal turns white in winter, except for the black tip of its tail. The white fur with spots of black was much admired, and from the reign of King Edward III (1327–1377) onward, only the royal family was allowed to wear it in England. Scarlet cloth trimmed in ermine was later adopted by European dukes as part of their ceremonial dress.

Princes of the Church

The Roman Catholic Church—which split from the Orthodox Church of the Byzantine Empire in 1054—was at the height of its power during this period. To most western Europeans, the popes in Rome were God's representatives on earth. They dressed in splendid robes and jewels, and wore a kind of crown as a symbol of their power. This papal tiara had evolved from the central part of the ancient Persian diadem and was worn by all popes from the ninth century. By the time of Pope Benedict XII (died 1342), the tiara was ringed by three crowns, arranged in tiers.

For religious ceremonies, the pope and all bishops wore a miter. This developed from a small crown with points at the side, worn in Asia. By

the end of the twelfth century, the miter had become a large, cloth-covered cylinder, embroidered and beribboned, which split into points at the front and back.

Monks and Nuns

Some objected to the earthly riches of the Church and preferred to live their lives in spiritual retreat. From the tenth century onward, these monks and nuns formed different "orders," communities devoted to a religious life. The orders favored very simple dress and each had its own uniform. The Dominicans wore white gowns and black caps. The Franciscans, who took a vow of poverty, wore a brown habit with a cowl, or hood, and a girdle of rope, whose knots reminded them of their vows as monks. The Carmelites wore white and brown stripes, and the Carthusians wore white only. Nuns had simple habits with a cloth worn over the head. By day they wore a cloth covering for their head and neck called a wimple.

On Pilgrimage

Great cathedrals were built across Europe at the height of the Middle Ages. These and other holy shrines were visited by pilgrims in order to pray or ask for a blessing from a saint. Popular destinations included Rome, Jerusalem, Canterbury Cathedral in England, and the Cathedral of St. James at Compostela in northwest Spain. A typical pilgrim carried a staff and a satchel and wore a tunic, a travel-stained cloak, and a broad-brimmed hat for protection against sun and rain. Each shrine had its own small badge made of lead, which pilgrims could wear on their hats or cloaks to show where they had been. The badge for Compostela was a shell, the emblem of St. James.

This statue of St James is dressed as a Compostela pilgrim. Note the shell emblem.

Courtly Fashion

The fashions of royalty and nobility were by now a world apart from the everyday dress of common people.

Fashions changed repeatedly between the twelfth and fifteenth centuries, as wealthy young nobles experimented with outrageous costumes and hairstyles. Young nobles shocked their elders and were often criticized by the Church.

At the beginning of this period, men's robes were becoming longer and shoes were elongated, with pointed or curled toes. Hair, cropped at the back of the neck in early Norman times, was now worn far beyond the length of a woman's, and long beards came into fashion too.

Later, men's hair was worn much shorter, with a central part and no beard.

From the 1340s onward, noblemen's garments went to the other extreme, becoming shorter and shorter, with the exposed legs covered in fitted hose. One leg of the hose might be red, the other blue. Sleeves almost touched the ground.

From the 1360s, a wide gown with flared sleeves and a high collar also became popular. Known as a *houppelande*, it was gathered into pleats with a belt at the waist. Gloves were often worn by nobles. Hats were also now worn, from round caps trimmed with fur, to separate or collared hoods with a long point at the back, which could be wrapped around or tucked in.

Sleeves and Veils

Noblewomen's dress remained long throughout the Middle Ages, with a variety of tunics and fitted over-gowns, known as *bliauds* coming in and out of fashion. Some were lined with furs, and wool and silk of the finest quality became increasingly available. The luxury of the cloth might be shown off in a long train sweeping the ground behind the body, or in rich undergarments revealed through slashes and laces in the gown. Sleeves might be so tight that they had to be detached and resewn after each wearing. Women's hair might be rolled or braided and coiled around the ears. Hair was generally covered with a linen veil, and in the twelfth century the neck and chin were also covered by a cloth called a barbet. The two cloths were later joined to form a single head covering, the wimple. A net of silk or beads, often supporting a stiff linen veil held with pins, was popular in the late fourteenth century.

The Age of Romance

This was the age of "courtly love," a code of behavior that idealized the love of a knight for a usually married noblewoman. Courtly love dictated how ladies dressed and walked and

looked at men. All sorts of hidden meanings could be read into such details as the color of a dress being worn. A lady might give a sleeve or a scarf to a knight who offered to be her "champion" at a tournament.

The fashion for ladies to wear very high headdresses and hats began at the end of the fourteenth century and reached its most extreme forms in the fifteenth.

Sumptuary Laws

Decrees which regulate the spending of the consumer are called sumptuary laws. They were introduced in most European countries during the later Middle Ages in order to limit the purchase of luxury goods. The aim was sometimes to curb excess, but more often it was to prevent wealthy merchants' wives, or others, from dressing in clothes reserved for the nobility. A French decree of 1294 does both, banning ordinary people from wearing certain furs and jewels, and limiting the amount of clothes a lord or lady might buy in a year. However, the rising middle classes were so determined to show off their newfound wealth that such laws rarely had any lasting effect.

Villeins, Merchants, and Mummers

Peasant Dress

From the eleventh to the thirteenth centuries, there were few changes in the dress of the lower classes. Some were reasonably provided for, but most were desperately poor. Common laborers, or villeins, wore a knee-length tunic or blouse of homespun cloth with breeches and coarse hose. On their feet they wore shoes of cloth, felt, or leather, or gaiters or wooden clogs. Men of all classes wore a capuchon, a long hood which dangled at the back but fitted closely around the head, extending over the shoulders as a collar or cape. A round, linen cap, which could be tied under the chin and worn under another hat, was also popular. Poor women wore a long gown of homespun cloth and hose.

An English poem called *Piers Plowman*, dating from the late fourteenth century, describes a poor peasant family: the man wears rough clothes full of holes; his wife has bare, bleeding feet; and the baby is wrapped in rags. In fact, by that time, life was beginning to improve a little for some of the poorest people. The decline of the feudal system was leading to a freer life in western Europe and the payment of regular wages. The Black Death, a terrible plague that devastated Asia and Europe between 1347 and 1351, reduced the workforce to such a degree that the survivors had more bargaining power. Better-quality woolen and linen cloth, cloaks, hose, boots, or shoes were now more commonly worn.

Professions in Gowns

The merchants and middle classes tended to live within their means, and generally dressed more sensibly than their superiors. Doctors had to wear long gowns, while surgeons, who were seen as workmen with lower status, wore short costumes. Lawyers and university professors also wore gowns, and their students were expected to dress soberly too, even if they did sometimes brawl and drink too much wine.

A fourteenth-century English manuscript, the Luttrell Psalter, shows farmers wearing belted tunics, hoods and brimmed hats.

Jugglers, Jesters, and Actors

One group of people who chose to wear brilliant colors were traveling acrobats, jugglers, and musicians. From the twelfth century onward, when fairs began to sell a wider variety of fabrics, entertainers began to wear multicolored outfits in bright red, yellow, and blue. They were blamed for spreading a taste for such outfits at court. Such garish costumes (known as "motley") became the uniform of the jester, a joker who was paid to fool around and make fun of people in the great hall of the castle. Jingling bells were attached to his cap.

There were no theaters at this time, but religious shows called miracle plays were often performed outdoors. The actors—all men or boys—were elaborately costumed as angels, devils, saints, and martyrs.

May Day and Mummery

There were many religious festivals during the Middle Ages, including some pre-Christian celebrations. On May Day, both nobles and peasants would wear green or adorn themselves with leaves and flowers, and dance to the music of bagpipes, drums, or fiddles. Carnival, the period before the fast of Lent, took on many of the customs of an old Roman winter festival called Saturnalia, during which servants and masters swapped roles. Revelers, known as mummers, banged drums and wore masks and grotesque costumes. They mocked the upper classes, dressing a goat as a bishop to preside over the "misrule."

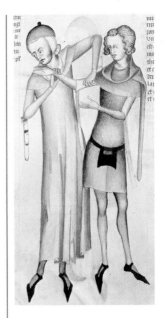

A doctor demonstrates how to take the pulse. He wears a cap and a long gown, as a mark of his profession.

Mummers shown in a fourteenth-century Flemish manuscript.

e gentki nonaer le uouli a auranore·

Knights and Foot Soldiers

Hauberks and Coifs

In the 1060s the Normans, who were based in northern France, invaded the British Isles and southern Europe. The Norman knight wore a hauberk, a knee-length coat of mail weighing about 30 pounds (14 kg), over a padded tunic. His head was protected by a mail hood, or coif, and a conical helmet with a nasal. Metal points called spurs, for urging on his horse, were strapped to his heels.

Coats of Arms

During the Crusades, Christian knights in the Middle East adopted the Muslim Saracens' habit of wearing a surcoat. This light over-garment helped protect the armor from heat and dust. Emblems on the surcoat identified the knight. Crusaders joined religious orders, like those of the monks. One of these, the Knights Templar, wore a white surcoat with a black cross. The Hospitallers wore a red surcoat with a white cross.

Across Europe, surcoats began to carry the emblem, or charge, of the wearer's family. The garment became known as a coat of arms. A code of rules was developed to regulate the colors, patterns, and emblems used. These rules were known as heraldry, for it was the task of a royal official called a herald to identify knights by their charges. Colorful and elaborate heraldic patterns also appeared on shields, standards, and the clothes of retainers and servants.

Plate Armor and Great Helms

By the thirteenth century, the knight's legs, hands, and feet were also covered in mail. Mail was effective, but it could still be pierced by arrowheads or smashed by maces and axes, so knights began to strap on plates of hardened leather or steel for further protection. By the 1400s, beautifully made and jointed plate armor of steel, weighing about forty-five to fifty-five pounds (20–25 kg), often covered the whole of the knight's body.

The helmet changed too. By the 1200s it was a flat-topped cylinder with the nasal extended to protect cheeks and eyes. By 1250 it was the

A thirteenth-century manuscript shows knights clad in mail and surcoats. Four knights in the background wear the great helm.

The Tournament

The mock battle, or tournament, began as a way of training knights. It included free-for-all fighting (the mêlée) and one-to-one horseback contests, in which one rider had to unseat the other with his lance. Tournament armor was heavier than field armor, and more padding was worn underneath. Even so, this was a dangerous sport. Knights began to wear more fanciful armor at tournaments, their helms decorated with crests, plumes, scarves, and ribbons. It was the knights' chance to achieve fame and fortune, and perhaps even a good match in marriage. The ladies of the court watched from pavilions and galleries, dressed in all of their finery.

great helm, a large, bucket-shaped helmet, padded inside and covering the whole coif. Slits and holes in the helm allowed for vision and breathing. As plate armor developed, so did a close-fitting, all-enclosing helmet called the basinet. From about 1300 this was fitted with a movable visor, which could be raised for improved vision.

Fighting on Foot

Foot soldiers and archers still wore simple tunics and hose, but many gained protection from padded jerkins or from mail shirts, armor, and helmets plundered from the battlefield.

In the 1300s there were major uprisings by peasants in western Europe. They were armed only with farm implements, knives, and homemade weapons, and had little armor. Their rebellions were easily and harshly suppressed by the knights.

An illustration of about 1340 shows an English knight, Sir Geoffrey Luttrell, being handed his jousting helmet, lance and shield before a tournament. His family coat of arms appears on his surcoat and his horse's trappings.

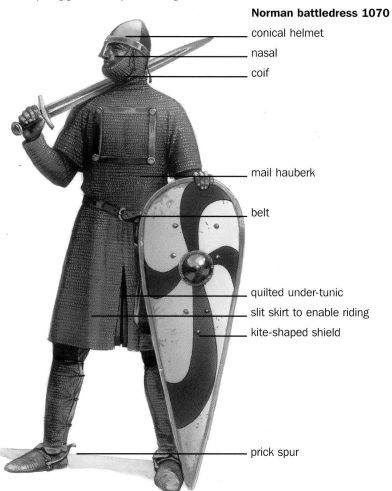

Norman battledress 1070

- conical helmet
- nasal
- coif
- mail hauberk
- belt
- quilted under-tunic
- slit skirt to enable riding
- kite-shaped shield
- prick spur

The Renaissance

Renaissance means "rebirth." Historians use the term to describe the revival of learning that took place in Europe toward the end of the Middle Ages. The scholars of the day looked back to the literature of ancient Rome and Greece for their inspiration, but this was also a time of looking forward: the start of the modern world. The Renaissance was at its most exuberant in the small city-states of Italy and across southern Europe, but it influenced the north as well.

Italian gentleman and lady, 1540

Men of Action

This was an age of great artists, architects, sculptors, poets, and inventors. They celebrated human beauty and intelligence. Their patrons, often rich bankers and princes, were individualists with a love of fashion and finery. At this time, the gowns and tunics of the Middle Ages gradually gave way to clothes which, chiefly for men, offered greater freedom of movement.

Nations and Trade

The Byzantine Empire fell to the Ottoman Turks in 1453, and this led to an increasing adoption of Asian costume, such as a broad tunic called the caftan, in eastern Europe.

In western Europe it evolved into a garment called the *caban*, which was the first form of coat.

The fifteenth and early sixteenth centuries were an age of exploration. The Portuguese sailed around Africa, opening up new trading routes to India and Southeast Asia, and new sources of imported textiles. Christopher Columbus, an Italian in the service of Spain, sailed to the Americas in 1492. Trade was about to be organized on a global scale. Within centuries, this would transform the production of fiber, the textile trade, and the kinds of clothes worn around the world.

Fifteen Thousand Tailors

The Renaissance period offered a wider range of textiles—imported or homemade—than had ever been available in Europe previously. There were woolens, silks and taffetas, brocades, velvets, damasks, fustians, cottons, and felts. The city of Milan alone had 15,000 tailors. By the early sixteenth century, looms were the most complex machines used in manufacture, and linen had become very fine. Women learned how to separate the threads into delicate patterns, making early forms of lace.

Palaces, Popes, and Protestants

The traditional long costume and mantle were still worn at the coronations of European kings and queens in the fifteenth and early sixteenth centuries, and the various regalia appear on coins of the day. The courtiers at the enthronement of the elected doge (chief magistrate) of the republic of Venice shimmered with silk, damask, and cloth of gold, the most costly fabric of the day. The *doge* himself wore an embroidered horn-shaped cap rather than a crown. Venice derived its wealth from maritime trade, and each year the doge would throw his official ring into the waves as a symbol of the "marriage" between Venice and the sea.

A 1434 painting by Jan van Eyck shows the dress worn at the wedding of wealthy Italian merchant Giovanni Arnolfini to his wife Giovanna.

Costume in Art

The Renaissance produced many great artists. The patrons who paid for the paintings loved to see themselves displayed in the very latest fashions. Even Biblical subjects were painted in the costumes of the day. *The Procession of the Magi,* painted by Benozzo Gozzoli in 1459, shows the full splendor of a Renaissance court, and includes portraits of the Medici family, the rich bankers who ruled the Italian city of Florence. Renaissance artists delighted in capturing the quality of silks, velvets, and pearls on canvas. Some, such as Antonio Pisanello (c. 1395–1455) and Jacopo Bellini (c. 1400–1470) went further and designed textiles themselves. They could be seen as the first fashion designers.

Isabella of Portugal, wife of Holy Roman Emperor Charles V, wears pearls, jewels, velvet, and lace in this painting of 1548.

Palace Fashions

In this age of moneymaking, most kings and other rulers dressed to display their wealth, rather than the old symbols of state power. Castles were beginning to grow obsolete during the later fifteenth century, partly as a result of the increasing firepower of cannons, which could breach the thickest walls. By the 1500s, fine royal palaces were being built instead, their walls hung with rich tapestries, as a splendid setting for the endless fashion parade of the royal family and the court. Fifteenth-century centers of high fashion included the royal courts of France and Spain, the court of the dukes of Burgundy, and the city-states of Italy, such as Florence, Venice, and Milan.

Not all kings were obsessed with fashion. Henry VII of England (reigned 1485–1509) was thrifty and preferred simple dress. However, his son Henry VIII (reigned 1509–1547) loved to show off the latest fashions as he danced and played music at court. He was a handsome youth, but as he grew older he became very fat, and the measurements for his costumes and armor became much wider.

The Church Divided

During the Renaissance period, the papacy came under the control of the same wealthy families that ran the Italian city-states. Popes were often very worldly, and richly jeweled rings and embroidered capes and robes became part of Church ceremonial dress.

In the 1500s the Catholic Church came under criticism from Protestants in northern Europe, for

Field of the Cloth of Gold

One of the most ostentatious displays of royal wealth took place at an encampment of lavishly furnished pavilions near Guines, in northern France, in 1520. Even the fountains spouted wine. The young King Henry VIII of England, and his first wife Catherine of Aragon, were guests of King François I and the French court. Each member of the royal party vied with the others in wearing the most extravagant costumes, furs, pearls, and jewels. The event became known as the Field of the Cloth of Gold. The expense nearly bankrupted both countries, but to no avail— they were soon at war with each other.

being corrupt. Protestants despised the wealth and rituals of Rome. They liked their own churches to be plain and simple, and this was the fashion of their clothes, too: simple black cloth and plain, white collars. When Henry VIII quarreled with the pope during the 1530s, the English king broke with the Catholic Church and closed down the monasteries. Monks in their habits disappeared from England, as they also did elsewhere in Protestant northern Europe.

The Heights of Fashion

During the fifteenth and sixteenth centuries, short costumes became increasingly fashionable among young men, although their fathers preferred to wear long gowns. Knee-length or calf-length garments, often with very long, fancy sleeves, also went in and out of fashion.

Doublet and Hose

The doublet was a padded jerkin, which derived from the protective garment worn under a knight's hauberk. It was close-fitting and waisted, made of rich brocades and trimmed with fur. In the 1400s the doublet was generally very short, revealing the full length of the leg, clad in hose. Virility was often emphasized and exaggerated with a codpiece. In the 1500s noblemen wore puffed sleeves, slashed to show the rich, silk lining. "Trunks," or short breeches, now appeared, and by the 1530s these often reached the knee. Short cloaks also became popular at this time.

Dressed in rich robes, Pope Leo X (1475-1521, a member of the powerful Medici family) is flanked by his cardinals, who wear red as a sign of their office.

Poulaines

Between the 1390s and 1460s, shoes for both men and women became even more pointed than in earlier centuries. This style was believed to have originated in Poland, and the shoes were known as *poulaines* or *crackows* (that is, from the city of Krakow). The points could be up to four inches (10 cm) long, and it is said that in 1396, French knights at Nicopolis had to cut off the points of their shoes before they were able to run away from their attackers. For wet and muddy streets, wooden soles, or pattens, could be tied onto the shoes. From the 1470s to the early 1500s, men's shoes became wide slippers with rounded, sometimes puffed, toes.

A pair of *poulaines* from the fifteenth century mark the extreme of medieval courtly fashion.

High Hats

Many kinds of headgear were worn by noblemen, including brimmed hats of velvet with fur trimmings, round caps, and tall cylinders. In the 1500s a flat cap of felt was worn, often adorned with plumes. A strange "pudding-basin" haircut was popular for men in northern Europe in the 1400s, while Italian dandies of the high Renaissance wore their hair long and curled. In the 1500s most men wore their hair short, with beards.

If noblemen's hats of the 1400s were thought to be outlandish, the women of the court were accused by priests of being in league with the devil. This was because fashionable hats worn at this time had twin points like horns. Even more extraordinary was the hennin, a tall, conical hat like

High headdresses and hennins were popular amongst noble women in the early fifteenth century.

a steeple, which supported a fine veil. By 1418 these hats had become so high that the doorways of Vincennes Castle, in France, had to be raised so that ladies could pass through them. In Italy too, women's hair was piled high, often with the addition of artificial hairpieces or extensions.

The Female Form

Noblewomen were obsessed with fashion during the Renaissance era, and the Church attacked them for wastefulness and vanity at a time when many people were poor. Priests also complained of indecency, as women's necklines plunged lower and lower. Italian women wore cosmetics and carried them, with a mirror, in a small purse. Their eyebrows and faces were plucked. Fans became a fashionable accessory in the warm lands of southern Europe.

Textiles were at their most beautiful at this time, and dresses were decorated with gems, ribbons, braids, embroidered hems, lace, and pearls. The noblewoman's undergarment was a chemise of silk, while the gown was tightly bodiced and laced, the skirt sometimes flowing out behind to form a train. The sixteenth century look included puffed sleeves, often slashed. Bodices were wired to emphasize a narrow waist. By the 1530s some women wore a high, lacy collar, which some years later developed into the ruff. The headdress was no longer high, and was made up of a head cloth, or bonnet and veil.

A late fifteenth–century manuscript shows a noble couple setting off to hunt with falcons on a fine May morning, riding two-up. He wears a low-crowned hat, a short doublet and riding boots. She rides side-saddle because of her long gown.

Fastening Clothes

For most of the Middle Ages, clothes were fastened with ties, laces, ribbons, pins, or brooches. Buttons were originally no more than a decoration: a small knob or ornament or piece of raised cloth, often appearing on a woman's dress. Buttons were occasionally matched with a cord loop and used as fasteners, and this function became more common in the fifteenth century, when buttons gained high-fashion status. Buttons have remained popular as fasteners ever since.

Everyday Costume

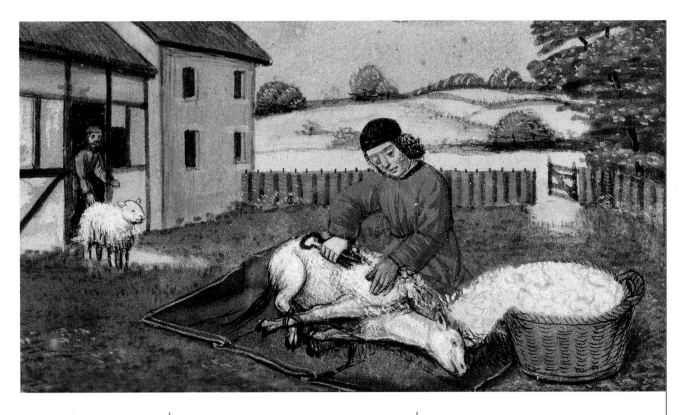

A Flemish illustration of the late fifteenth century shows a farm laborer shearing sheep in June. Woolen cloth was an important part of the economy in northern Europe.

The extreme fashions of the court in the fifteenth century were not designed to be practical. They celebrated the fact that nobles did not have to engage in manual work. Everyday dress for ordinary people in town and in the country was much more simple.

People at Work

The laborer of fifteenth–century Europe wore a thigh-length tunic or shirt of wool or linen, often colored brown, green, or blue. A simple belt around the waist would be hung with a money-pouch, a water bottle, a knife, or perhaps a container for a stone, used to sharpen his scythe at harvest time. Linen hose might be rolled down to the knees or tucked inside his boots. Collared hoods and wide-brimmed hats of straw or felt had changed little from the previous century. In the 1500s boots and shoes became broader and more rounded, as with the gentry.

Children with baby c. 1450

An ordinary woman of the town or country might wear a long, colored gown, with sleeves which could be unfastened at the cuff and rolled up for hard work, such as washing clothes. The outer skirt might be tucked up into the waistband of a petticoat or kirtle. This was a separate under-skirt of coarse cloth, seamed at the back and gathered into a waistband. A white apron was often tied around the waist. Sometimes a separate short-sleeved over-garment of linen or knitted wool would be worn, similar to a modern sweater. Hair might be tied up in a cloth or kerchief, or a simple headdress of stiff linen which aimed to imitate the more elaborate versions worn by women of the upper classes.

Middle Classes

The costume of the middle classes was less showy than that of the nobility, but their garments were made of the best-quality cloth. A long, fur-trimmed gown might be worn by a wealthy wool merchant or a scholar. Older people who were farsighted might now be seen with spectacles held in their hands or perched on their noses. Spectacles had probably been invented in the later thirteenth century. Younger middle-class citizens began to wear shorter and shorter tunics during the fifteenth century, sometimes buttoned down the front.

The wives of wealthy citizens could also afford fur trimmings and might have fancy, colored cuffs or necklines even if they did not own the fabulously rich fabrics of the royal court. The style of dress and the caps, hoods, and headdresses imitated courtly fashions also, but were much more conservative. Low necklines or tight lacings were not considered proper for the respectable wife of a merchant or public official.

These are wealthy citizens of the fifteenth-century merchant class. Their clothes are of good quality and imitate the fashion of the court.

Growing Up

Newborn babies of all social classes were tightly wrapped in bands of linen or wool, before being laid in a cradle or basket. These "swaddling clothes" were believed to keep babies warm and safe, and to help their limbs to grow straight. Children did not have their own styles of dress, but wore scaled-down versions of the adult dress of their day. Their simple tunics allowed plenty of freedom to run around and play—or to work, for country children were expected to help out on the family farm from a young age.

The Grandest Armor

skull

brow reinforce

upper bevor

lower bevor

rondel

gorget plate

vambrace

rest

pauldron

cowter

breastplate

skirt

tasset

rump guard

gauntlet

cuisse

poleyn

greave

Full plate-armor, early fifteenth century

sabaton

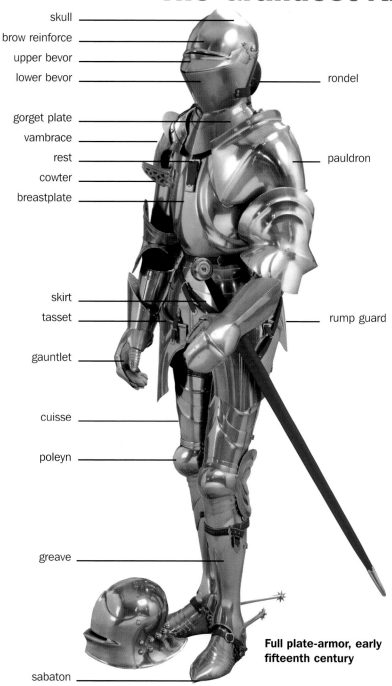

The metalworking skills of European armorers peaked in the 1400s and early 1500s. European towns which specialized in the manufacture of armor and weapons included: Solingen, Nuremberg, Passau, and Augsburg in Germany; Innsbruck in Austria; Milan in Italy; and Toledo in Spain. Paris was the center of armor-making in France, as London was in England. Armor was stamped with the trademark of each city's guild and of the armorer himself. The best armor was made-to-measure and was very expensive.

Full Plate Armor

A knight of the early fifteenth century wore linen hose and a padded doublet with mail sections to protect vulnerable parts of the body. Having dressed in these, the knight (with the help of his squire) strapped on leg armor, secured with laces, and armored shoes, or *sabatons*. The upper body was covered with a backplate and a breastplate, and the arms were also covered in padded plate sections. Then came the *pauldrons*, or shoulder pieces, the gorget to protect the neck, and the armored gloves, or gauntlets. The helmet, which enclosed the whole head, was put on

Dress for a Gunner

By the 1470s handguns were already playing an important part on the battlefield. Guns were slow to load and very unreliable, so being a hand-gunner was dangerous work. During this period the gunner might strap a breastplate over a mail shirt and wear a brimmed, open helmet (known as a kettle hat) over a collared hood. He would wear hose and boots. A dagger and a pouch would probably hang from his leather belt, and a powder horn to hold gunpowder might be slung on a cord across one shoulder.

last. The whole suit of armor was finely jointed to allow easy movement.

Fancy Styles

Different styles of armor developed in the later fifteenth century. Italian armor tended to be rounded and smooth, while German armor in the Gothic style was elongated and fluted, with long, pointed sabatons. Plates were often brass-edged. Another style, which historians call "Maximilian armor," appeared between 1510 and 1530. It had heavily ridged plates designed to deflect blades, and squared-off sabatons. The grandest armor of all was designed to be worn by Renaissance kings and princes on parade or at a tournament. Italian parade armor was often elaborately decorated in gold and silver, and embossed with fantastic patterns and designs. Similarly splendid armor was made for the rider's horse.

Changing Times

The high point in armor manufacture was reached in the sixteenth century, but already the nature of warfare was changing, as artillery and then handheld firearms became common and more effective. Mobility and vision were increasingly important on the battlefield, and three-quarter or half suits of armor became more practical for knights as well as foot soldiers.

During the 1500s the Spanish conquistadors—the soldiers who conquered indigenous peoples in the Americas—wore only a single cuirass (a piece of armor to protect the upper body) and a brimmed helmet, which left the face open.

This scene, painted by Paolo Uccello in the 1450s, shows Italian mercenary armies fighting in the battle of San Romano (1432). The knights wear full plate armor.

Chapter 4: Africa and Asia 500–1550

Old Worlds

China's chief trading route for textiles, the Silk Road, passed through Central Asia. These Chinese statues, from eighth-century Xian, show Central Asian musicians on horseback.

Many of the garments used across the Western world today, from trousers to coats, originated in the East, in the continent of Asia. For most of the medieval period, Asian lands possessed the most advanced textile technology in the world, pioneering sericulture (silk production), spinning wheels, and treadle looms. Asia produced the world's finest and most beautiful materials, and these were being exported to Europe, by land and sea, long before the start of the medieval period. The spread of Asia's weaving skills was encouraged by movements of peoples, by merchants and travelers, and even by contact between warring armies.

These musicians wear costumes from the early part of China's Song dynasty (907–1276). This was a golden age of arts and crafts, in which silk production reached a new level of perfection.

Asia in the Middle Ages

The greatest empire in medieval Asia was that of China. The Chinese believed that their homeland lay at the center of the civilized world. Chinese cultural influence in the medieval period extended into Korea, Japan, and Vietnam, and there was also Chinese contact with India, Arabia, and even East Africa. Western Asia was greatly influenced by the spread of the Islamic faith by the Arabs during the early Middle Ages. Meanwhile, in southern India, powerful Hindu kingdoms arose, whose influence extended into Southeast Asia. In the later Middle Ages, Central Asian peoples such as the Turks and Mongols gained control of vast areas of Asia, including northern India.

Wild animal motifs have great tribal and spiritual significance in African costume. This arm ornament takes the form of a leopard.

Africa in the Middle Ages

In the early medieval period, the faith of Islam was carried westward through Egypt and the rest of North Africa by conquering Arab armies. In Algeria and Morocco, Arab culture fused with that of the native Berber people, becoming known as "Moorish," and moved on from there into southern Spain. The Moors traded southward across the Sahara, influencing the indigenous empires of West Africa. At the same time, Arab and Persian merchants sailed down the coast and islands of East Africa, where a cultural fusion with local peoples created the "Swahili" culture. In northeast Africa, the ancient Christian kingdom of Ethiopia took its traditions and religions from the Coptic Church of Egypt, rather than Islam.

The interior of the African continent also had powerful kingdoms and tribal federations with their own cultures and beliefs. Many were founded by ironworking farmers, the Niger-Congo peoples, who expanded southward and eastward from their western-central African homeland before, during, and after the medieval period. Other areas were populated by peoples who lived by hunting and gathering food, such as the so-called Pygmies of the rainforests and the Khoi-San peoples of southern Africa.

Henna in Asia and Africa

Henna is an Asian shrub, and in ancient Turkey its leaves were dried to make a powdered dye, in orange, red, or black. With the Islamic expansion in the early medieval period, the use of henna as a cosmetic spread across North Africa into Moorish Spain, southward along the coasts of East Africa and through much of the Middle East. The dye was used to trace elaborate patterns on women's hands or feet, a custom associated with religious festivals and marriage celebrations. The finest henna decorations appeared in the Middle East between about 900 and 1550, as evidenced from pottery and paintings of the day.

Sub-Saharan Africa

The chief centers of textile production in medieval Africa were Egypt and the northwest, or Maghreb. In the chiefdoms and kingdoms to the south of the Sahara Desert, the textiles, body decorations, and costumes were often very striking.

In the West African kingdom of Benin, masks like this one were worn at the hip by rulers during certain ceremonies.

Wearing Masks

In West and Central Africa, masks were worn for all kinds of religious rituals, such as fertility or harvest dances, coming-of-age ceremonies, and funerals. The masks mostly represented spirits rather than human forms. They were made of carved and painted wood, feathers, raffia, shells, fur, ivory, or metal and usually formed part of an elaborate costume.

Beyond the Sahara

As trade expanded southward across the Sahara during the Middle Ages, camel caravans brought cottons and silks to the rising states of West Africa. The arrival of Islam in this region brought with it flowing robes in the Arab style. Native textile industries developed in the medieval city-states of the Hausa people, in Ghana, and in the Mali and Kanem-Bornu empires. A uniquely West African weaving tradition evolved in these places, in which strips of beautifully patterned cotton are sewn together.

Kano, a Hausa city founded in 999 CE, soon became famous for its cotton textiles and also for its leather, exporting hides to the Maghreb. Its medieval dye pits, which used indigo to color the dark blue cotton robes of desert traders, still exist today.

On the East African coast and islands, people also adopted Arab cotton robes, wove cloth, and imported Asian textiles from across the Indian Ocean.

Fur, Hide, and Raffia

Across Africa, people wore or traded the pelts of wild animals, such as leopards. The bravery and status of warriors might be emphasized by headdresses made of lion manes or other evidence of hunting prowess. Short kilts, tunics, and cloaks for both sexes were often made of wild animal or cattle hides. The bark of certain trees could be soaked and beaten into a fine cloth. Grasses, leaves, and fronds, such as those of raffia palms, were used to make skirts or other simple coverings.

Body Art

Many African hunters and gatherers went naked most of the time, but decorated their bodies, faces, or hair with reddish earth (ocher) or white wood ash. It is clear from surviving medieval statues and carvings that the decorative scarring of faces or bodies was widespread. The marks often indicated status, sex, clan, or tribe. Teeth filed to a point were a mark of beauty to some peoples, as extended earlobes were to others.

Necklaces and Anklets

Necklaces, collars, earrings, armbands, and anklets were commonly used across medieval Africa. They might be made of copper, gold, iron, ivory, bone, wood, or cowrie shells. Copper was the most highly valued metal in the early Middle Ages, later overtaken by gold.

Royal and Ritual Dress

Many African rulers wore or carried regalia to indicate their royal status. These included elaborate headdresses, feathers and plumes, crowns, scepters, collars or necklaces, gourds, and weapons. African religion was based on a belief in spirits of nature and magic, and in honoring the spirits of one's ancestors. Traditional curers, guardians of shrines, ritual dancers, or members of secret cults often wore special costumes and masks, representing the power of birds, animals, or spirits. The costumes might be made of straw, feathers, hide, or fur. Boys and girls undergoing rituals to mark the coming of adulthood also had to wear special costumes, body decorations, or headdresses.

Cloth is still dyed with indigo in medieval pits at Kano, in what is now northern Nigeria. This Hausa city, founded in 999, was a center of textile production in the Middle Ages.

The Arab World

During the Middle Ages, the Arab world stretched from Spain through North Africa and the Middle East. Textiles were woven by desert nomads as well as in the cities, and cloth was one of the most important trading items. Fabrics included wool, cotton, linen, and silk, and Morocco was famous for its leatherwork.

In this portrait, a Libyan horseman in the desert is robed much as his medieval ancestors would have been.

Moorish Andalusia became a source of rich silk textiles used in regalia and vestments in southern Europe.

Influences on Dress

Two main factors influenced Arab dress. One of these was climate. Heat and desert sand encouraged the wearing of loose-fitting robes, often white to reflect the sun, and of veils or scarves to protect the head and face. Cotton was the ideal fabric for such clothing. However, during cold nights and windy or wintry weather, woolen robes or cloaks were also worn.

The other factor influencing Arab dress was the Koran, or Islamic scripture. The Koran orders men to dress modestly, with tunics no shorter than the knee and no longer than the ankle. Women were also expected to dress modestly in loose robes. Fitted clothes, jewelry, and tattoos were frowned upon.

Damask and Muslin

The influence of the Arab world on textiles is shown in words we still use for certain types of fabric. Damask takes its name from Damascus, in Syria. It is a reversible fabric made most often of silk or linen. A pattern is woven into the cloth which is revealed by the way in which light falls upon the fabric. Muslin takes its name from Mosul, a town in present-day Iraq. It is a fine, gauzy cotton.

Men's Dress

Arab men might wear loose, knee-length breeches as underpants, beneath a long tunic. Sleeves could be wide or narrow. Over this might be worn a jacket or an open-fronted robe called an *aba*. Sleeves for both men and women were often sewn with a decorative band called a *tiraz*. At first these were worn only by caliphs (rulers), but later they were adopted more widely. They were often embroidered with religious inscriptions, calling down the blessings of God upon the caliph. Hair was worn short, and older men always wore a beard. A skull cap was worn on the head, and around this would be wound a long turban.

Arab warriors in the Middle Ages often wore tunics and boots. Over this they might put on a quilted, padded jacket or perhaps a shirt of mail or scale armor. A cotton robe (the "surcoat" adopted by European knights) was sometimes worn over everything. A conical helmet, often with a turban wrapped around it, protected the head. A leather belt carried the sword.

Women's Dress

Arab women also wore loose tunics and robes, sometimes over tight trousers. The practice of wearing a veil varied greatly from one region to another. It might conceal part or most of the face, or simply be a scarf over the head. In some regions the veil was worn at all times outside the house or among strangers, to protect the wearer's modesty. In others, Muslim women only wore the veil for worship.

Non-Arabs

The lands of the Muslim Arabs were also populated by other peoples, such as the Berbers and Kurds, who wore much the same clothes as their Arab neighbors. The Persians tended to favor more luxurious silks and jewelry than the Arabs. Jewish citizens tended to wear the dress of the region in which they were living. Jews and Christians living in Muslim lands were sometimes ordered to identify themselves by wearing turbans of a particular color.

This woman wears the costume of the Ottoman Turkish court at the end of the medieval period. Unlike most Arab women, she is unveiled.

Turks and Mongols

A Seljuk Turkish warrior preparing to shoot an arrow from his lightweight bow.

The steppe grasslands of Central Asia were home to the Turkic-speaking peoples and tribes. One Turkic group, the Seljuks, ruled large areas of western Asia from the eleventh to the thirteenth centuries. They were followed by the Ottomans, Muslim Turks who seized land from the Byzantine Empire. By the end of the medieval period, the Ottoman Empire included large areas of the Middle East and North Africa.

Turkish Warriors

Like all Central Asian warriors, the Seljuk Turks were great horsemen and archers. Illustrations show them wearing knee-length breeches and pointed slippers, quilted jackets, shirts of mail or scale armor, sashes, and round caps. They carried small bows and quivers of arrows, round shields, and a kind of slashing sword which developed into the saber.

Veils and Sultans

In the fourteenth century the Moroccan explorer Ibn Battutah was shocked to find that Turkish women did not wear the veil and were entertained alongside their menfolk.

Felt Making

Felt, which was ideal for keeping out cold winds, was one of the most important fabrics for the medieval Mongols. First, the sheep were washed and sheared, and the fleece was then combed out or carded, and possibly dyed. The wool was spread over a mat of reeds and sprinkled with hot water, then rolled up in the mat and tightly bound. After hours of rolling, the bundle was unpacked. The wool, now densely compacted, was dried and could then be cut and sewn into tunics, jackets and coats, hats, boots, and bags. Felt was also made into rugs and blankets, and was the cloth used for the round tents of the steppes, known as yurts.

This tradition had remained from before their conversion to Islam.

As rulers of the great Ottoman Empire, the Turks indulged in luxury. Sultans of the sixteenth century, such as Suleyman the Magnificent (reigned 1520–1566), were neatly bearded and wore huge turbans on their heads. They had splendid tunics, and robes with elbow-length sleeves. The men and women of the royal court wore cottons, silks, brocades, taffetas, and velvets, mostly produced in the town of Bursa.

Riders of the Steppe

The greatest conquerors of medieval Asia were the Mongols, who lived on the steppe grasslands of Central and Eastern Asia. Their first great leader was Temujin, or Genghis Khan (c. 1162–1227). Mongol armies conquered much of Asia and the Middle East, as well as parts of eastern Europe.

Mongol armies included horseback archers, and light and heavy cavalry. Warriors wore fur or sheepskin caps with long earflaps, or plumed, conical helmets made of hardened leather or metal, with armored flaps to protect the neck. Tunics of wool or silk, trimmed with fur, were worn in conjunction with armor, which was made from small plates of iron or lacquered leather, laced together in strips.

Mongol Dress

The basic item of everyday dress for both men and women was a long, collarless caftan known as a *del*. The front overlapped to the right and was fastened with five ties. It was generally blue, red, or yellow—a color later reserved for Buddhist priests. Men wore the *del* over loose trousers and high boots. Women wore it longer, over underskirts. Men and unmarried women wore a broad, colored sash around the waist. Both men and women braided their hair, with men also shaving parts of their head. Those descendants of Genghis Khan's warriors who ended up living in luxury in China or Persia wore expensive silks and furs, and eventually adopted local costume.

Mongol archer on horseback.

Southern Asia

In India, saris of cotton or silk were worn together with beautiful necklaces, bracelets, anklets, earrings, and nose rings.

In the 1930s, freedom campaigner Mohandas K. Gandhi adopted the simple spinning wheel, whose design had not changed since the medieval period, as an appropriate symbol of India's history and way of life. Cotton was grown in the Indus valley (now in Pakistan) in prehistoric times. The Indian subcontinent (all the land south of the Himalayan mountain ranges) was the center of world cotton production throughout the Middle Ages. Silks, originally a Chinese invention, were also made in medieval India. Indian skills in dyeing and patterning textiles were legendary.

Saris and Dhotis

Several items of Hindu dress, none of which were cut and sewn, were in use throughout the ancient, medieval, and modern periods, and continue to be worn today. One example was the sari, worn by Indian women, which took its name from the Sanskrit word for cloth, *chira*. It was made of silk or cotton, often in dazzling colors. This rectangle of cloth, between thirteen and twenty-six feet (4–8 m) in length and about fifty inches (120 cm) wide, was wrapped around the waist and then folded into pleats (known as *plati*), and tucked into the waistband. The rest of the sari (the *pallu*) was draped over the shoulder. The breasts were supported by a band of cloth tied at the back (later, the *choli*, or blouse). A petticoat (*ardhoruka*) was first worn under a sari in the medieval period.

The dhoti was the male equivalent of the sari, being an ankle-length cloth wound around the waist. The *lungi* was a simple cotton loincloth. All these clothes were ideal for the Indian climate and could be tucked up to make them shorter for work in the fields. Veils and turbans in various styles have provided head covering throughout Indian history.

The Delhi Sultanate

Traditional unsewn garments were worn in northern Hindu kingdoms of the early Middle Ages. However, the Muslim rulers of the Delhi Sultanate, which controlled northern India from the thirteenth to the sixteenth centuries, were set apart from most of their subjects by their tailored clothes, trousers, long-sleeved tunics, and skirts. Many of these were made of splendid textiles, worked with gold. Hindu and Muslim weavers worked alongside each other in the royal workshops, and the techniques and styles of the two cultures influenced each other.

Southern Kingdoms

Southern India remained under the rule of Hindu kingdoms, some of which extended their influence across parts of Southeast Asia. Temples supported craftworkers' guilds and workshops. These produced beautiful jewelry and the finest textiles for the royal court and also for the ritual dancers who performed in the temples. Southern Indians still favored fine, draped clothes which accentuated the human figure. Rank was shown by the quality of the cloth rather than by difference of costume. Even kings went bare-chested.

This painting shows the court of Babur (1483–1530), first Moghul emperor of India. Moghul dress was influenced by Mongol, Persian and Indian costume traditions.

Coat of a Thousand Nails

Wars between Hindus and Muslims in the Middle Ages were fought with infantry and archers, heavy and light cavalry, and elephants. The Muslim armies in the north did employ some Hindus, but were largely made up of non-Indians. They wore the mail shirts and scale armor of Central Asia and the Middle East. The native Hindu tradition was to wear light armor, such as a caftan (known here as a *kubcha*) of padded cloth. However, the Indians learned from their enemies, and by the end of the Middle Ages their kaftans included the armored "coat of a thousand nails," which was patterned with protective studs.

Imperial China

Although China suffered setbacks and invasions during the Middle Ages, from the eleventh to the thirteenth centuries it enjoyed a period of economic prosperity, flourishing art and literature, and technological advances. Its riches in the 1270s astounded the Venetian traveler Marco Polo. Costly bales of textiles were bought and sold along the Silk Road, a network of trading routes which extended from China to the Middle East.

Chinese Fabrics

Silk production, or sericulture, was China's most famous invention. Silkworms (caterpillars of the silk moth) were placed on trays and fed with mulberry leaves. They produced cocoons, and when these were plunged into hot water, the fine filaments came apart and could be reeled off and twisted together to make silk thread. Chinese silk-making probably reached its zenith during the Song dynasty (907–1276).

Codes of Dress

The teachings of Kongfuzi or Confucius, which were already a thousand years old at the outset of the Middle Ages, emphasized social order, hierarchy, and duty. These concerns were reflected in dress codes. Silk was the textile worn by emperors and empresses, by members of the imperial court, and by government and military officials. Color and patched motifs such as animals or birds indicated rank. Chinese religious traditions emphasized visual harmony,

This statue from China's Tang dynasty (581-907) shows a lady of the court wearing an elegant silk gown with long sleeves and an elaborate hairstyle.

This picture shows an emperor and empress from China's Ming dynasty (1368–1644). Note the long sleeves of the silk robes.

so symmetry, or balance, was also an important element of fashion design. Ankle-length silk costume was the formal dress for both men and women during most of the medieval period.

The most common form of gown worn by important men was the *pao shen*, a long silk gown generally worn over trousers which were tucked into boots. Women's fashion at the imperial court included a narrow-sleeved everyday gown and a ceremonial gown with enormously wide sleeves.

Changing Fashions

Chinese women's fashions varied over the years. There were long

Little Feet

During the tenth or eleventh centuries, a custom began among families of Chinese dancers and entertainers. At the age of five or six, young girls had their feet tightly bound. This prevented the foot from growing naturally and caused severe deformation. The intention was that when they grew up, their feet would look tiny and that they would trip along daintily as they walked. Later, in the Song dynasty, this cruel practice became a general fashion, which lasted into modern times. A pair of women's embroidered slippers of the thirteenth century, discovered in Fujian province, were just five inches (13 cm) long.

gowns or long skirts worn beneath tunics, sashes and shawls, crowns and headdresses, higher or lower necklines, collars or no collars. The most colorful period for women's fashion was during the prosperous Tang dynasty (618–907), when noblewomen still led fairly active lives.

Farmers and Soldiers

Working people such as farmers, laborers, or even merchants, were forbidden from wearing silk gowns. In the cold north, furs and sheepskins kept people warm. In the warm south, cotton tunics were worn over loose trousers, with sandals made from straw or rushes. Chinese soldiers wore armor of scales, small plates, leather, or—from the twelfth century—bands of iron. A unique type of armor was invented in the Tang dynasty, made from up to fifteen layers of glued paper. It was surprisingly tough.

Non-Chinese Fashions

The Yuan dynasty, founded by Mongol conquerors in 1271, brought Mongolian influence to bear on male and female fashion, such as very wide waistbands. However, the Mongols eventually adopted Chinese clothes.

A painting of 1280 shows the dynasty's founder, Kublai Khan, wearing rich Chinese brocades beneath his Mongolian furs.

Korea and Japan

China's neighbors to the east included the Koreans and the Japanese. There was plenty of interaction between the various cultures, especially in costume and fashion.

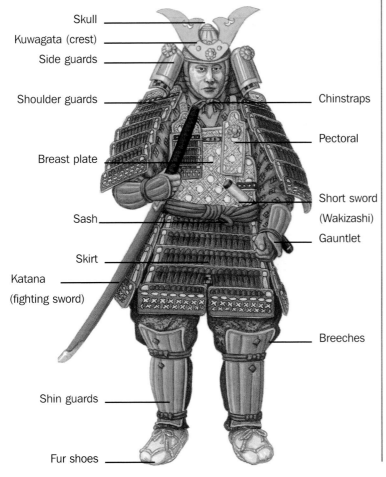

A medieval Japanese *samurai* dresses for battle in the full *o-yoroi*.

Skull

Kuwagata (crest)

Side guards

Shoulder guards

Breast plate

Sash

Skirt

Katana (fighting sword)

Shin guards

Fur shoes

Chinstraps

Pectoral

Short sword (Wakizashi)

Gauntlet

Breeches

Korean *Hanbok*

The Korean peninsula, extending from the Chinese mainland, was occupied by three small kingdoms at the start of the Middle Ages: Gogureyo, Silla, and Baekje. Power shifted between the three. A new dynasty, the Goryeo, ruled until the Mongols invaded in the 1270s, after which the Joseon kingdom was founded.

Korea's quite bulky-looking traditional dress (*hanbok*) dates back to the Three Kingdoms period. It originated as a caftan-style garment, worn by both men and women, closed right to left and fastened with a belt. This eventually evolved into a short jacket, the *jeogori*, tied left-over-right (the Chinese way), with a long ribbon. Below this, women wore a long, wraparound skirt, the *chima*, also fastened with ribbons. Men wore baggy trousers beneath the jacket, gathered in at the ankles. A long coat called the *durumagi* might also be worn. In the Joseon kingdom, as in China, colors of dress indicated rank and status.

Feudal Warriors

Medieval Japan developed a feudal system similar to that of Europe. Its feudal lords were called *daimyo*. They wore *eboshi*, black caps of silk stiffened with lacquered paper, over a topknot of hair. Their knights were called *samurai*, and they formed a social elite, following a strict code of honor (*Bushido*). *Samurai* warriors developed elaborate and very fine armor between 858 and 1185. The *o-yoroi* (great armor) combined plate sections with strips of small, lacquered plates laced together with tasseled silk cords, wide shoulder guards, and skirts. It was worn over robes and breeches. The bowl-shaped helmet had a broad, flared neck flap and crest. Fully armed, the mere appearance of the samurai struck fear into their enemies.

Japanese Costume

Eastward from Korea lay the mountainous islands of Japan. Here, craft skills had been practiced since prehistoric times: Japan has the oldest known pottery in the world, and silk and hemp cloths were being produced at an early date. At the start of the Middle Ages, the Japanese nobility wore long, silk costumes, either as two separate garments or as a one-piece gown. Chinese fashions were closely followed. Sumptuary laws issued in 718 even insisted that robes should be fastened in exactly the same way as in China.

In the ninth and tenth centuries, Japan began to grow away from Chinese influence. Robes for men and women of the imperial court, cut to a straight-line pattern and then sewn together, mark the origins of the dress that in modern times has become known to the Western world as the *kimono* (a word which actually just means "clothing"). Robes could be worn in several layers. Colors denoted the status of the wearer and varied with the seasons.

From 1185 emperors lost control to the nobles and wars raged through Japan. Fashions became much simpler and more austere at this time, but luxury and color returned at the end of the medieval period. The modern *kimono* style did not appear until after the Middle Ages.

Wraparound robes were worn by many social classes, in cotton, hemp, or ramie, if not silk. Working men wore tunics over loose trousers and sandals of straw or wooden-soled shoes. Shoes were never worn indoors. Splendid costumes and beautiful masks were worn by actors in a type of drama called Noh, which became popular from the 1300s onward.

In Noh theatre, males played female parts, and wore masks like this one.

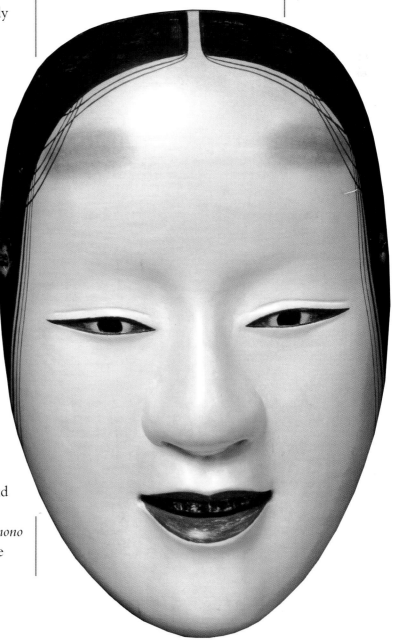

Oceania

There is no record of Europeans reaching Australia before 1606, although it is possible that a Chinese fleet reached its shores in the fifteenth century. However, the Australian aborigines had populated the continent perhaps 50,000 years previously. During the Middle Ages, the Aborigines formed scattered groups of hunters and gatherers across the land.

The vast expanse of the Pacific was not crossed by Europeans until Ferdinand Magellan's fleet entered that ocean in 1519. However, its countless islands had been colonized by Southeast Asian peoples such as the Melanesians and the Lapita folk (ancestors of the Polynesians). Polynesian migrations took place between about 1000 BCE and 1000 CE. By the 1200s the Polynesian islands were ruled by powerful chiefs. The islands and larger landmasses of the Pacific Ocean were not visited by outsiders during the Middle Ages. There are no written accounts of how Australian aborigines or Pacific islanders looked or dressed at this time. However, later traditions and archaeological remains offer some evidence. For example, huge, carved stone figures were raised on Easter Island during the Middle Ages. Some of the stone heads have elongated earlobes. Some have earplugs, red topknots, and what may represent tattooing and loincloths.

The mysterious Easter Island statues give us some clues about the appearance of Polynesian rulers in the Middle Ages.

Australian Hunters

Australia's aborigines were experts at surviving in a harsh, hot environment. They lived by fishing, hunting, and gathering, and also sowed and harvested seeds of food plants where

Polynesian Tattoos

Our word *tattoo* comes from the Tahitian word *tatau*. The practice of tattooing is found across the Polynesian islands and was common during the medieval period. Archaeologists in New Zealand have dated a *uhi* (the chisel or burin used to make the tattoos) to sometime between 1150 and 1260. Tattooing customs varied across the Pacific, but the patterns were always very elaborate and had spiritual and social significance. The Maori tattoo, or *moko*, covered a warrior's whole head (the most sacred part of his body), and sometimes also his thighs, with swirling lines. Maori women might tattoo their lower face, around the mouth.

possible. The aborigines mostly went naked, but in many regions they wore sewn cloaks of kangaroo or opossum skin, pinned at the shoulder. On the island of Tasmania they greased their bodies with animal fat as protection against the cold.

The aborigines wove, knotted, coiled, and dyed fibers such as long pandanus leaves. They made bags, headbands, armbands, pendants, necklaces, bracelets, and pendants, using shells, bones, animal teeth, claws, feathers, and fur. Bodies were decorated with ocher or ash and cut to produce decorative scarring. The geometrical patterns on their bodies reflected their beliefs in ancestral animal spirits and clans, and they made elaborate headdresses for religious ceremonies and dances. In some regions hair was dressed with red ocher; in others it was decorated with seeds. Men were often bearded.

Across the Pacific

The Melanesians, Micronesians, and Polynesians who populated the Pacific islands in the medieval period generally made use of grasses, leaves, and fronds to make kilts or longer skirts. Shells, bones, and flowers were worn for ornament. A tradition developed of making garments from a barkcloth fabric known as *tapa*. The pithy inner bark of the paper mulberry tree was stripped away, soaked, and beaten until flat. It was then dried, and sections were glued together, dyed, and cut.

Facial tattooing was common amongst the Maoris of medieval New Zealand and other Pacific islanders.

Cloaks have a long tradition in Maori history, worn by chiefs and representing the honor of the family or clan. They were generally woven by older women.

Maori Flax and Feathers

The last of the great Pacific migrations was carried out by the Polynesian ancestors of the Maori people, who probably arrived in New Zealand by canoe toward the end of the tenth century CE. New Zealand was colder than many other Pacific islands, and the islanders had

Hine-Rehia

Weaving played such an important part in medieval life that it appears time after time in mythology and folklore around the world. In New Zealand, folk tales of the Polynesian Maori people tell how the first settlers on the islands learned how to use local plants for weaving. They tell of Hine-Rehia, a fairy woman, who knew all the secrets of preparing, working, and dyeing the local form of flax. She would only work by night, saying that daylight would destroy her beautiful work. Local women decided to learn the secret for themselves. They used trickery to keep her up during the day and spied on her as she worked. She realized too late, and with a wail was carried away on a cloud. The Maori women now knew how to prepare and plait the flax and make fine cloaks all day long. Hine-Rehia was never seen again, but was sometimes heard wailing in the night, lamenting the loss of her secret.

to adapt to a life in a new environment. One of the most valuable native plant fibers was *harakeke*, or New Zealand flax. Other textile fibers came from a climbing plant called *kiekie*, and many plants produced natural dyes. Twined cords were worn around the waist, supporting a woven or plaited short kilt. Women did not always cover their breasts, and men went into battle naked.

The Maoris wore cloaks made of flax fiber cloth or the skins of dogs. They also developed a technique for decorating the finest cloaks with masses of feathers, most commonly of the kiwi. The feather cloak, or *kahu huruhuru*, was a prized possession, handed down from one generation to the next.

Necklaces of bone and whale tooth were worn, and, later, pendants and long earrings of greenstone and other materials became popular. Carved combs were worn in the warrior's topknot, sometimes with a feather.

The Americas have been peopled since prehistoric times. By the medieval period, great empires had grown up in regions of South and Central America,

while in North America tribal peoples lived by hunting or farming.

The 700s CE saw the rise of Pueblo cultures, with villages built of adobe (sun-dried mud brick). In the later Middle Ages, these villages were built into the sides of cliffs and canyons. These defensive sites were abandoned, probably as a result of drought and warfare, in the fourteenth century. The three main Pueblo cultures are known as Hohokam, Mogollon, and Anasazi.

The southwest of North America has a dry climate, which has preserved fragments of fabrics, feathers, and fibers. Coarse fibers such as yucca were used to make sandals and clothing, sewn with bone needles and thread made of animal sinews. Simple loincloths were worn, or tunics and blankets made from hides and furs. Cotton was cultivated from about the year 1000.

Textiles played an important part in the life of the Anasazi farmers.

Textiles were dyed with plants such as sumach, or minerals such as ocher or iron oxide. They were painted with geometric patterns, or sometimes decorated with embroidery. Jewelry was clearly influenced by Mexican styles and was made of shell, turquoise, or feathers.

Medieval Mississippi

The first towns in North America appeared in the 700s CE in the Middle Mississippi valley and reached their high point in the thirteenth century. In 1200 the town of Cahokia had a population of about ten thousand. The Middle Mississippians were successful farmers, and also hunted with bows and arrows.

Surviving Mississippian artifacts include masks of wood and shell, copper pendants, and gorgets—engraved shell disks worn on the chest. Carved images show dancers dressed in masks and feathers. Textiles were made by twining methods rather than true weaving, and were then dyed. They were traded over a very wide area, and were made into cloaks, skirts, and bags. The regional climate is humid, so only a few textile fragments have survived. Clothes were also made from hide and furs.

Tattoos and Topknots

The influence of the Mississippians extended into the woodlands of the northeast. Here, the ancestors of the Iroquois peoples learned to clear land and farm, but they were also hunters. Northeastern dress was mostly of buckskin or furs. A short cloth was worn by men to cover the loins, and a fringed skirt by women. The bare upper parts of the body were often tattooed and adorned with necklaces,

Native Americans of the east coast wore few clothes and often tattooed or painted their bodies and shaved their heads.

armbands, or porcupine quills. Men's heads were mostly shaven, leaving a topknot or crest. Faces might be painted.

Red Cedar and Dog Wool

The Pacific coast peoples of the northwest lived by fishing, and hunting whales and seals. Their chief source of fiber was the red cedar tree. Long strips of the soft bark were cut each summer. These could be woven on upright looms and made into blankets or skirts. Another source of fiber was the wool from their fluffy dogs. Cedar bark was also made into conical hats, to keep off rain or sea spray.

Arctic Survival

Waves of settlers from Siberia, such as the Aleuts and the Inuit, had peopled Arctic America in prehistoric times. Migration and settlement continued through the medieval period, eastward to Greenland. Clothes were made from the hides of caribou, musk ox, polar bear, or arctic hare or fox, and from bird skins and feathers. Hides were softened by chewing or beating and sewn with gut to make tailored, close-fitting layers. These included breeches for both men and women, shirts, hoods, gloves, and boots to protect against wind chill and frostbite.

Civilized cultures had populated Central America long before the Middle Ages. Great cities flourished during the medieval period, such as Teotihuacán, near Lake Texcoco; the Mayan city of Chichén Itzá; and the Aztec capital, Tenochtitlán.

Maguey and Cotton

Few medieval fabrics have survived in the tropical climate of the region, but clothing styles and textile processes are revealed in stone carvings and pottery, in Mayan wall paintings, and in Aztec illustrated sheets called codices. Native dress was also described by the conquering Spanish.

This codex sheet lists tribute goods paid to the Aztec rulers by 26 towns in their empire. Goods provided include civilian clothes (top), battledress and war shields (center).

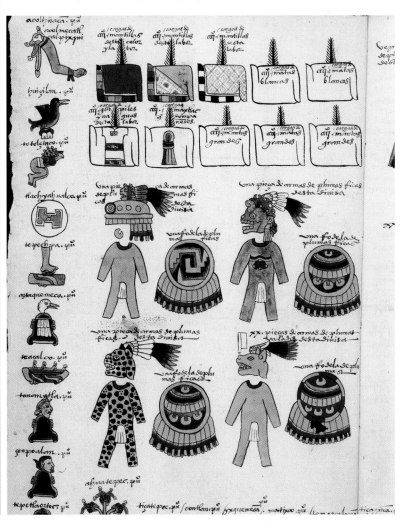

Feather Work

Some of the most skillful craftworkers were the Aztec *amanteca*, or feather-workers. They were part of a longstanding tradition in the region. Brilliantly colored feathers from wild or specially bred tropical birds were tied into fabric as it was woven. Feather work was used for headdresses, ceremonial shields, and the splendid cloaks worn only by royalty and the nobility. A headdress was sent from the Aztec ruler Montezuma II (reigned 1502–1520) to the king of Spain. It was made of gold, turquoise, and the shimmering green feathers of the sacred quetzal bird.

Aztec quetzal feather headdress, early sixteenth century

Aztec dress styles were strictly regulated according to rank.

Textiles, garments, jewelry, and feathers often meant much more than mere items of clothing or adornment. A marriage ceremony was marked by the symbolic knotting together of the clothes worn by bride and groom. Clothes and textiles were also sent by subject peoples as tribute—a kind of tax—to the Aztec emperors.

Spinning was done with a drop spindle, and weaving on backstrap looms. Cactus spines were used as needles for sewing. The most common fibers in the region came from tough desert plants such as maguey agave. The fibers were coarse, but could produce a surprisingly flexible cloth, worn by most ordinary people. Cool, smooth cotton was cultivated in warm, lowland areas from the start of the Middle Ages. Amongst the Aztecs, it was reserved for nobles in accordance with strict sumptuary laws.

Dyes were made from minerals, plants, and animals. Purple was obtained from shellfish, and crimson from cochineal insects, collected from cultivated groves of nopal cactus. Textiles were patterned with geometric designs, flowers, or animals, or decorated with embroidery.

Clothes and Jewelry

Clothes worn in the region were not close-fitting. Loose

garments were favored, such as tunics, loincloths, skirts, and women's blouses (*huipils*). Cloaks were knotted around the neck. The design of the clothes varied little, but the quality of the cloth indicated social status. However, even nobles had to wear simple cloaks when in the company of the emperor. Mayan paintings show lords dressed in jaguar skins, plumes, and ritual headdresses.

Jewelry included ear plugs, lip plugs, earrings, and necklaces. Many of the finest jewelers were Mixtecs, and they worked in shell, amber, obsidian, jade, turquoise, and gold. An Aztec emperor wore armbands, anklets, and rattles of gold on his feet. To the Aztecs, gold and silver were sacred metals, associated with worship of the Sun and Moon and with the emperor and empress. Commoners were not allowed to wear precious metals or gems.

Men wore their hair short, and boys wore a long tuft of hair at the back. Unmarried women wore their hair long, but married women braided their hair around the head, so that two bound "horns" stuck out on each side. A young woman might paint her face yellow or use clay stamps to pattern her skin with dyes.

Warriors and Priests

Warriors wore elaborate costumes. The Aztec army had two elite units, the Jaguars and the Eagles, whose uniforms were designed to look like these creatures. Helmets were made of bone or wood and armor was of padded cotton. The Aztec priests, who performed human sacrifices, painted their faces and bodies black and never washed their hair.

This statue from Tula shows the battledress of a Toltec warrior. The Toltecs were at the height of their power between the tenth and twelfth centuries.

South America

At the start of the Middle Ages, the Andes mountains and Pacific coast of South America were home to various cultures. In 500 CE the city of Tiwaniku, near Lake Titicaca, may have had a population of up to 100,000 people. The city-state of Wari reached the height of its powers in about 700 CE, at a time when the ancient coastal civilizations of Moche in the north, and Nazca in the arid south, were coming to an end. The Chimú civilization was growing up in the city of Chan Chan and was a major power by 900 CE.

The feather headdress and ear plugs signified high rank amongst the Chancay people of the central Peruvian coast in the late medieval period.

The last of the great Andean civilizations was Tawantinsuyu, the empire of the Incas. Their capital, Cuzco, in modern Peru, was founded in about 1100. The Incas built up their empire until it extended 2,230 miles (3,600 km) north to south, and about 200 miles (320 km) inland. It was invaded by Spanish troops in the 1530s.

Cotton and Camelids

Medieval South America had a very ancient textile tradition. Cotton was widely grown and as a cool fiber it was popular in the hot, coastal regions. Camelid wool was also prized. The llama had a coarse coat, but the alpaca and wild vicuña produced yarn of the highest quality. Plants and cochineal insects provided dyes.

Drop spindles were used, as they still are in the Andes. The upright loom was traditional in some regions, and was best for making broad strips of cloth, but the backstrap loom was the most widespread. Needles were of bone, and embroidery was common. Patterns included animals, flowers, and geometric motifs. The finest textiles—worn by rulers, nobles, or priests—might include beautiful feathers, gold work, sequins, or beads.

Women of all social classes learned to weave, and there were male weavers, too. In the Inca empire, textiles were collected as part of a tax that all households had to pay, and were stored in government warehouses.

Inca Dress

Inca men wore a simple, belted loincloth beneath a knee-length poncho-style tunic, often made of alpaca wool. A cloak would be worn during cold weather. Women wore a rectangular alpaca wrap, tied by a sash at the waist, and a shawl. The *tupu*, a long decorative pin in copper, silver, or gold was used to fasten wraps, shawls, and cloaks. Sandals were made of leather or grasses.

There were many regional variants of headgear, from headbands and woolen caps to feathered headdresses. Headdresses indicated rank in the Inca army. The crown of the Inca emperor was the *llauta*, a multicolored braid with tassels and gold pendants.

Gold and Silver

The Moche and Chimú peoples produced beautiful gold jewelry, and the Andean peoples loved to wear necklaces, pendants, nostril rings, and disks. Jewelry was also made from shell, from local turquoise or imported jet, and lapis lazuli. Only nobles were allowed to wear precious metals. Large gold ear plugs were an emblem of noble rank.

This Chancay textile is elaborately decorated with zigzag patterns and beads.

Beyond the Andes

To the east of the Andes were the vast rainforests around the Orinoco and Amazon rivers. Here, the peoples went naked or wore leaves and fibers, or skins. They painted their bodies with tribal markings. Little is known of dress in the far south of the continent at this time, but the native Fuegians probably appeared much as their descendants did, with matted hair and faces painted in red, black, and white. They wore cloaks of another wild camelid, the guanaco, and rubbed animal grease into their bodies as protection against the cold.

Timeline

CE

527	Justinian the Great becomes Byzantine emperor. He founds silk workshops.
600s	Royal costume and regalia is adopted in western Europe, influenced by the Byzantine Empire.
618	The start of the Tang dynasty in China: at this time there is a thriving textile trade through Central Asia along the Silk Road.
c. 625	Sutton Hoo grave goods include gold buckles and an ornate helmet, artifacts of Anglo-Saxon England.
718	Sumptuary laws are issued in Japan.
c. 800	The Tara brooch. The height of late Celtic jewelry-making in Ireland.
800s	Vikings trade in Russian furs, Asian textiles, and jewelry.
858	The beginnings of Samurai armor in Japan.
c. 900	The high point of henna decorative design in the Middle East (to c. 1550).
c. 900	The growth of the textile trade in Islamic North Africa.
907	The Song dynasty in China: the height of elegance in fashion (to 1276).
957	The Bruges cloth fair. The rise of Flanders as a center of textile production, reaching its height in the 1300s.
999	The founding of Kano, a center of the West African textile trade and dyeing.
c. 1000	The colonizing Maoris learn to use local fiber plants in New Zealand.
c. 1000	Cotton is first cultivated in North America.
1035	A Chinese illustration shows a spinning wheel.
c. 1100	Treadle looms are used in Europe.
1100s	Long costume is worn in Europe.
1100s	The founding of the Inca empire in South America: alpaca and cotton textiles.
1100s	Guilds are established by European weavers and tailors.
1100s	Crusader kingdoms are established in the Middle East, leading to an Asian influence on European dress.
1206	The Delhi Sultanate: Muslim dress is introduced into northern India.
1220s	Metal plates begin to be added to mail armor in Europe.
1276	The Mongol conquest of China: the adoption of Mongolian dress styles.
c. 1280	The first spinning wheels appear in Europe.
1294	Sumptuary laws are issued in France.
1320s	Lace is first made in France and Flanders.
c. 1340	The rise of the short costume in Europe.
1390s	Extremely pointed shoes (*poulaines*) become popular in Europe (until the 1460s).
1400s	Renaissance artists design textiles: the world's first "fashion designers."
1400s	Full plate armor is being worn in Europe.
1400s	The Aztec empire, at the height of its power in Mexico, employs Mixtec craft workers.
1418	"Steeple" hats (*hennins*) are at their highest at the royal court of France.
1500s	Ornate parade armor is produced in Italy and Germany.

Glossary

backstrap A type of loom in which the warp threads are tensioned by a belt around the weaver's waist.

barkcloth Any fabric produced from the bark of various trees, as used in some Polynesian, African, and Native American cultures.

bobbin A spool or reel from which yarn can be dispensed.

brocade Any rich fabric with an elaborate, raised pattern woven into it.

capuchon A hood with a long point dangling at the back.

card To comb or disentangle wool, flax or other fibers before spinning.

charge The emblem or badge of a noble family.

coat of arms (1) A surcoat emblazoned with the family emblem of its owner. (2) The badge of a noble family.

codpiece A padded pocket fitted to the front of tight-fitting men's hose or breeches.

coif Any head covering, especially the mail hood worn by a knight.

cowl A large hood attached to the robes of a monk.

damask A reversible, patterned fabric made of linen, silk, cotton or wool.

diadem A cloth headband set with jewels, used as a crown in ancient Persia.

distaff A cleft stick, used to hold raw fiber which is being spun into yarn.

doublet A padded jerkin.

drop spindle A whirling, suspended rod and whorl, used to spin yarn.

finger weaving One of various techniques for weaving by hand without a loom.

flax A family of plants whose fibrous stems are stripped out to make linen.

fustian A sturdy, short-piled cloth made of linen warp and cotton weft.

habit The uniform robes worn by a monk or nun, of any religion.

hauberk A knee-length coat of mail.

heddle A bar on a loom which positions the warp threads so that the weft may be guided through them.

hennin A tall, pointed, steeple-like hat worn by European women in the 1400s.

homespun A simple cloth that has been woven in the home or which is made of yarn that has been spun in the home.

hose The common form of leg covering for men and women in medieval Europe.

houppelande A flared style of gown worn by men and women in medieval Europe.

kerchief A piece of cloth, used as a scarf or head covering.

kettle hat A helmet taking the form of a brimmed iron hat.

loom Any kind of frame used to tension threads during weaving.

mail A form of armor, made up of interlinked rings of iron.

mantle A loose cloak, without sleeves.

muslin A fine cotton gauze.

nasal The part of a helmet which protects the nose, generally a metal bar.

orb A globe, carried as part of regalia.

pattens Wooden attachments to the soles of shoes, designed to keep them out of the mud.

pendant Something that hangs from something else, such as side pieces of a crown or an ornament hung around the neck.

plate armor Armor which covers the wearer in fitted sections of metal.

poulaines Extremely long and pointed shoes.

regalia Clothes, crowns or other emblems used by a ruler as an emblem of rank.

sari A cloth of cotton or silk, wrapped in pleats around the waist and draped over the shoulder.

scale armor Small platelets of metal or leather, attached to a garment.

scepter A staff carried by a ruler as a symbol of authority.

sericulture The raising of the caterpillars of certain moths ("silkworms") in order to make silk textiles from their cocoons.

Further Information

shed The gap made in the warp threads on a loom, so that the weft can be passed through.

shuttle A piece of wood which carries the weft thread through the raised warp threads on a loom.

sumptuary laws Laws which regulate the consumer, especially those declaring which clothes may be purchased.

surcoat A light garment worn over armor.

swaddling clothes Bands of linen or wool in which babies were once tightly wrapped.

tapestry A textile on which pictures or patterns have been woven into the warp threads.

taffeta A glossy, plain-woven form of silk.

train A long extension to the hem of a dress, trailing behind the wearer.

treadles Foot-operated levers which control the heddle on a hand loom.

velvet A soft, thick-piled fabric of silk and/or cotton.

warp The long or upright threads tensioned by a loom for weaving into textiles.

weft The cross threads passed between the warp during weaving.

whorl A disc which keeps the spindle turning evenly during spinning by hand.

wimple A cloth covering head and chin, worn by European women in the fourteenth century.

Adult General Reference Sources

Brooke, Iris, *English Costume from the Middle Ages through the Sixteenth Century* (Dover Publications, 2000)

Garrett, Valery M., *Chinese Clothing: An Illustrated Guide* (Oxford University Press, 1994)

Houston, Mary G., *Medieval Costume in England and France in the Thirteenth, Fourteenth, and Fifteenth Centuries* (Dover Publications, 1996)

Norris, Herbert, *Medieval Costume and Fashion* (J. M. Dent and Sons, 1927; reissued by Dover Publications, 1999)

Peacock, John, *The Chronicle of Western Costume: From the Ancient World to the Late Twentieth Century* (Thames and Hudson, 2003)

Pfaffenbichler, Mattias, *Medieval Craftsmen: Armourers* (British Museum Press, 1992)

Staniland, Kay, *Medieval Craftsmen: Embroiderers* (British Museum Press, 1992)

Stilman, Yesida Kalfon, and Stilman, Norman A., *Arab Dress: A Short History from the Dawn of Islam to Modern Times* (Brill Academic Publishers, second revised edition, 2003)

Young Adult Sources

Dawson, Imogen, *Clothes and Crafts in Aztec Times* (Gareth Stevens Publishing, 2000)

Dawson, Imogen, *Clothes and Crafts in the Middle Ages* (Gareth Stevens Publishing, 2000)

Internet Resources

http://www.costumes.org/history/100pages/greeklinks.htm

A general website on the history of costume with links to sites on different cultures and their costumes.

http://www.costumes.org/history/100pages/medievalinks.htm

Medieval Costume links page within The Costumer's Manifesto site.

**http://www.costumegallery.com/
Medieval.htm**
Links to websites on all aspects of medieval
costume, covering the period 100–1499 CE.

**http://www.ravensgard.org/gerekr/
costumef.html**
Ravensgard Costume Page. Contains over a
hundred links to Medieval Costume Resources.

**http://www.pipcom.com/~tempus/tempus/
index.html**
Tempus Peregrinator's Web Page. A personal
site by a reenactor who has detailed
information on medieval clothing, most notably
the Houppelande, but also pages of useful
information for those wishing to replicate it for
stage or reenacting.

**http://www.geocities.com/kaganate/clothing.
html**
The Red Kaganate. Images and information on
Central Asian clothing of the Middle Ages, with
patterns.

http://www.reconstructinghistory.com
Reconstructing History Pattern Company.
Commercial site with large sections of site
devoted to free information about Medieval and
Renaissance dress in Japan, Ireland and
Scotland.

**http://www.personal.utulsa.edu/~marc-
carlson/cloth/bockhome.html**
Some Clothing of The Middle Ages. Well-
researched site on rare Medieval European
clothing from archeological digs.

http://www.virtue.to/articles/Index.html
Medieval Clothing Pages. Articles by Cynthia
Virtue include both detailed history and
extensive how-to information for making modern
replicas.

http://www.arador.com/main/index.html
The Arador Armor Library. Information on both
plate and chain mail armor.

**http://www.geocities.com/karen_larsdatter/
foolwear.htm**
Foolish Clothing. Depictions of Jesters and
Fools in Medieval and Renaissance Art

**http://hometown.aol.com/Predslava/
GiliarovskaiaPatterns.html**
Patterns and Instructions for Medieval Russian
Costumes.

http://www.gryph.com/byzantine/dress.htm
The Basics of Byzantine Dress c. 1000 A.D.
Includes pictures of surviving garments.

**http://www.nativeweb.org/resources/crafts_
indigenous_technology/leather_clothing/
native_american_clothing/**
NativeWeb Resources: Native American Clothing
links to thirty-one sites on Native American
traditional dress.